Planning Your
Teaching Year

Planning Your Teaching Year

A CATECHIST'S GUIDE TO DEVELOPING EFFECTIVE GOALS

Monica A. Hughes

PAULIST PRESS
New York/Mahwah, NJ

Cover and book design by Lynn Else

Library of Congress Cataloging-in-Publication Data

Hughes, Monica A.
    Planning your teaching year : a catechist's guide to developing effective goals / Monica A. Hughes.
        p. cm.
    ISBN 978-0-8091-4569-0 (alk. paper)
    1. Catechetics—Catholic Church. 2. Catechists. 3. Catholic Church—Education. I. Title.
    BX1968.H85 2009
    268′.3—dc22

                                                    2008033675

Published by Paulist Press
997 Macarthur Boulevard
Mahwah, New Jersey 07430

www.paulistpress.com

Printed and bound in the
United States of America

Contents

Introduction

Recently, I purchased a hand-painted puzzle whose pieces were not interlocking or color-connected in the traditional way. There wasn't even a template on which to place the shapes. The only clues were that some of the pieces formed recognizable objects: a sun, a flower, an evergreen tree, a rainbow. The completed puzzle presented a colorful and beautiful butterfly.

I decided to test the age appropriateness of the puzzle with my two-and-a-half-year-old granddaughter. So we dumped out all the puzzle pieces and then attempted to reassemble them as a picture. It proved a bit difficult for her to decipher the proper placement of each piece, so I helped. Working together, we started with the outside edges and progressed toward the center of the puzzle. She needed guidance along the way, but eventually we were successful in re-creating the colorful butterfly.

Many new and even seasoned catechists will experience a similar challenge as they begin to prepare for a new teaching assignment. In order to guide their participants through the learning process, catechists effectively have to assemble a puzzle whose pieces include new groups, new teaching environments, and frequently changing resources and expectations. This guide is for the new catechist seeking guidance, for the seasoned catechist who recognizes the need for something other than a book of scripted lessons, and for all catechists who need to plan programs for children, teens, and adults. In short, this is a book for everyone who wants to develop a dynamic catechesis that is responsive to the local community.

Not to plan is to be lost, fragmented, confused, and confusing, running around in circles. But there is more than one way to plan. If you think of scripture, doctrine, time, resources, the program, and the community as pieces of the puzzle, this book can help you put them all together to form a living, vibrant picture painted by the Holy Spirit. Faith formation is a dialogue. If you as a catechist really want to engage your participants, you simply can't follow a text without deviation. You will be much more confident and effective if you have a framework in which to elicit dialogue while at the same time keeping within your plan. This book offers methods to enhance your resourcefulness and flexibility as you plan your catechetical year.

1
Beginning the Planning Process

So where exactly do you begin? The real beginning is in saying yes to the assignment. Paragraph 55B of the U.S. Bishops' *National Directory for Catechesis* (see chapter 2 for more on this important document) suggests that candidates for the role of catechist enter prayerful discernment with the leadership of their parishes or schools before making such a commitment. This discernment process is an essential step in collecting some of your puzzle pieces, because through it you will learn how much support there is for you within your faith community. As a catechist you are both representative of your community as well as responsible to it. You serve the community and it supports you. You cannot minister effectively as a catechist without taking time to develop a meaningful relationship with the members of your community—they are one of your most important resources.

This engagement with your faith community will help you to discern:

- Is this where I am being called to serve?
- Do I experience the presence of Christ here in such a way that I feel really able to share the gift of Christianity with others?
- Am I called to be a catechist in this particular faith community?
- What is the Spirit of God saying to me?

YOUR PRIORITIES AS A CATECHIST

So, God is calling you to teach. Here is a short values test to get a sense of what you believe is important for a catechist. Rank the following statements in order of importance from your point of view, where 1 is most important and 10 is the least important.

_____ Catechists take time to grow in their faith through study, prayer, and quiet time with God.

_____ Catechists know their participants and become aware of how they relate to each other.

_____ Catechists become a link with their parish communities and the Sunday liturgy.

_____ Catechists represent the church as mediators and interpreters of the faith.

_____ Catechists are facilitators of learning and encourage memorization.

_____ Catechists help their participants to connect life and faith, making that connection genuine and life-giving.

_____ Catechists pray with their participants.

_____ Catechists encourage Christian action as a response to faith, prayer, and discussion.

_____ Catechists engage in ministry of the word, a sharing of the scriptures.

_____ Catechists actively embrace teaching methods that reflect genuine respect for cultural diversity.

Look carefully at the statements you have ranked as 1, 2, and 3. Obviously, these numbers represent the most important values for you. It may have been somewhat difficult for you to make the choices for each assertion. This is because all of the statements collectively create a total picture of the many roles that a catechist plays within the church and parish.

ROLE OF THE CATECHIST

People who become catechists shine forth in the parish community in a very special way through the faith that they share. To sum up, let's name the different roles you will perform as a catechist in your faith community. As a catechist, you are a(n):

- Greeter—Your first responsibility is to help everyone in your class feel at home, safe, and cared for. Greet each person by name and with a smile. Your welcome conveys how much you value each person in the group.
- Faith-Sharer—In this role you not only give witness to your faith, but you also support opportunities for

others to share their faith, showing forth the marvelous work of God. In that sharing you will find that everyone's faith grows.

- Educator—Your lessons should help others learn about our faith. You will want to hand on the truths of the faith in such a way that the hearts of those listening are filled with love and joy. In this way their response becomes a living faith within each of their lives.

- Communicator—Your challenge is to convey your message to a specific group of people who are hungry to hear God's word. You need to use effective communication skills to meaningfully reach your group, whatever its age level. Remember not to do all the talking—God also works in silence, within the heart of each person.

- Integrator—It is your role to make the elements of your lesson relevant to the faith and life of your participants. Be attentive to what is happening in the lives of your participants so that you can integrate their experiences into your teaching.

- Leader—You not only direct learning activities but, more importantly, you give witness to your faith by the life you lead. When you lead your participants in prayer or accompany them to Sunday liturgy, your life becomes a model of discipleship for others.

These roles might surprise you, but when you accept the role of catechist, you take on a special responsibility.

You become more than yourself, a gateway through which others can experience Jesus Christ. You become an instrument that is used by God to lead others to Christ.

FINDING TIME

Having accepted your new role, you will find yourself facing a fast-paced world filled with constant interruptions. Jobs, parental responsibilities, household tasks, television, radio, iPods, newspaper headlines, ads, and commercial billboards all clamor for our attention. It seems that we can only communicate in sound bites and with cell phones, e-mail, fax machines, or computers. Your biggest challenge as a catechist may simply be finding a period of uninterrupted time for prayer and planning. Time is another piece that makes up the puzzle.

It might be helpful to create both a *weekly* and a *daily* task schedule, each one in the form of a wheel that resembles a pie-plate graph. First, draw two circles. Divide the first circle into six sections, each section representing one day of the workweek. This is your "week-wheel." Write in your tasks for the week, day by day, on the week-wheel— this will give you a good visual sense of which days are really busy and which days are less so. Next, select the best day for prayer and planning. The second circle will represent that day. Divide the second circle into eight hour-long sections. This is your "day-wheel." Use this wheel to determine the best hours of your selected day to devote to prayer and planning.

Don't feel obligated to keep rigidly to these schedules, but use them as tools to help you best utilize your time as a catechist. If, for example, you are months away from meeting with your class, you might only need to spend time every other week for long-range planning.

Spending regular time in prayer with God will change your life. You will find yourself more centered with a greater sense of meaning from within. Taking time for prayer is an essential part of being a catechist.

RESOURCES AND INFORMATION

You have made your decision to be a catechist. You have considered what this role means. You have committed yourself to taking the necessary time to perform this task well—and to do it with and for God. Now it is time to collect all the necessary pieces, though not in any particular order. You will need a variety of resources to effectively plan: information about participants and parents, class location, available supplies, support for duplicating copies, textbook resources, expectations for set-up and clean-up, spiritual and formation opportunities, parish information, disaster plans, descriptions of roles and responsibilities, authority structures, mentor-teachers, network support and guidance, and record keeping. And of course the liturgical seasons, the weekly scriptural readings, and the flow of sacramental preparation are also resources that fit into the puzzle.

It's time to consider all the things that you will need to learn.

Participants and Their Parents

- Who are they?
- What schools do they attend?
- What are their family situations?
- Where do they live?
- What is the cultural background of the families and how will that affect my teaching plans?
- What are their interests?
- Are they in any sports programs?
- How are the families involved in the parish?
- Do the participants that are coming already know one another?
- Have they been in the program before?
- Do they come to class hungry?
- Are they embarrassed by their family, their economic situation, or even their clothes?

My Class Assignment

- How many are enrolled in my class?
- What are their ages?
- When will I get a class list?
- How long will each lesson be?
- Will there be any parent support?
- What are the expectations regarding participant discipline?
- Whom do I contact in case of emergency?

Environment and Supplies

- Where will the class meet?
- Are there desks or tables in the room?
- Will I be able to move any of the furniture in the room?
- Who will unlock/lock the building/room?
- Does someone else use this room on a daily basis?
- Where is the electrical outlet?
- Will I need an extension cord?
- What is the lighting like?
- Does media equipment already exist in the room and if so, may I use it?
- Is there a chalkboard, white board, or bulletin board that I will be able to use?
- What supplies will be available for the participants?
- Where will the supplies be kept?
- Where can I set up a prayer space?
- Can I arrive early and get into my room to set up?
- What is the disaster plan for this setting?

Program Support

- Will the participants have a textbook?
- When will I receive the teacher manual?
- Are a yearly calendar and grade-level outcomes available?
- What books and audiovisual materials are available for use?

- How do I request the use of resources and equipment?
- What procedures are in place for general and classroom emergencies?
- Will someone act as a mentor catechist/teacher?
- Will there be additional meetings that I will need to attend?
- Who will clean up the room after my teaching session?
- What procedures do I follow if I suspect child abuse?
- How will I communicate with the parents?
- How will attendance records be kept?

The list of questions is not exhaustive. No doubt you can add several of your own questions to the list.

Add Your Questions Here:

MANAGING THE MANY DETAILS

All these questions may seem overwhelming. Here's a technique that will give you the confidence to manage them:

1. First, **check** all the questions for which you currently have the information.
2. Next, **circle** the questions for which you need immediate information in order to plan effectively.
3. Finally, place a **star** in front of the questions for which you will need the information, but not right away.

Collecting the information necessary for your assignment will be your first task. Place your collected information into a folder and set aside a place at home to keep the larger items together.

Rather than placing all your information in a pile, use an expandable folder with sections for days and months. This way you can file information for projects according to the dates by which they need to be completed. Because you have arranged your information by date, you can go through your folder regularly, working on projects little by little and moving project information to other files as needed. A date-based filing system can also be set up through Microsoft Outlook, which has an automatic reminder function. As long you keep Outlook updated, it will alert you to upcoming projects and lessons.

Each of the following chapters is designed to help you to plan for an effective year as teacher and catechist. As with any puzzle, there is more than one way to approach this planning process. The chapters can be consulted in any order. They contain ideas, templates, exercises, and processes that work well no matter how you arrange them. So you don't need to follow the chapters sequentially! Read whatever section addresses your needs at a particular time. You need to use all the pieces to assemble the entire picture, but it is up to you to put them together. As you plan your teaching year, you are also growing as a catechist. Welcome!

2
Discovering Your Context

A puzzle has boundaries, and many people find it easiest to assemble puzzles by beginning with the straight edges that form the outside frame. In a similar way, context is the frame that helps us make sense of a word, a passage, or an idea. Context refers to the whole set of interrelated conditions in which something exists or occurs. Context both limits and defines meaning.

Why does context matter in religious education? Because it creates meaning from what is woven together. We teach that life is not just about "me." One cannot understand that until one recognizes others around "me." Catechesis cannot take place in isolation. Neither can planning take place in isolation from all that surrounds you. Context is about relationships and the envelope holding those relationships.

THE LIVES OF YOUR PARTICIPANTS

The task of this chapter is to take a look at your situation and that of your participants. You must open yourself to the learner's context because it is important to teach in a way that is meaningful to the lives of your participants.

What they learn in religious education must connect to their life experience. Catechists teach through, with, and in the experiences of their participants—with the participants themselves, their families and friends, their community, their nation, and their world.

"What do you hope to accomplish?" is usually one of the first questions asked in any project. It is interesting that we begin our discussion for planning your teaching year in religious education by looking at context rather than goals and objectives. Fundamentally, religious education is both a journey and the story of our developing relationship with God. Relationship involves the "me" and the "you"— or in the case of the catechist, the "we" and the "you."

It's very easy to focus our religious education on the nature and being of God. But if religious education fails to explore the relationship of individuals and communities with God, it becomes just a philosophical exercise. If a lesson is mostly a lecture, then half the relationship is missing. God doesn't need religious education—but the people of God are nourished and enriched by it. So we must always keep in mind the people of God. It doesn't matter whether we are engaging with very sophisticated adults or the youngest of children. As a catechist, part of your preparation is to understand and explore the community you are engaging.

Imagine yourself hosting a party in honor of a very eminent person. Let's go all the way and host the pope. You know that he will be gracious and considerate, or he wouldn't be attending your party. All of your guests have heard of the pope, of course, but to most of them he is little more than a remote symbol. As the host of the party, you must introduce each of your guests to this special person and provide a little guidance to get conversations started. But how? You certainly don't want to just rave on and on about papal travels and writings and blessings. Nor would you bore the pope with the biography of all your guests. Rather, you would use your understanding of your guests to stimulate conversation, and then you would gracefully withdraw, allowing all your guests, including the pope, the space to engage with each other.

IMPORTANCE OF HUMAN EXPERIENCE

The dinner party metaphor invites you to explore the richness and diversity of human experience. It likens your role as catechist to that of a host at a party, where you invite people into the joy of a relationship with God. In a similar way, you bring yourself into a relationship with your participants. But for this to happen, you must also know yourself in your own context. So the rest of this chapter challenges you to discover yourself as you get to know your participants.

Are you feeling like this chapter is going to be too much? Is it sounding like you need to know everything about everyone, as well as all history, culture, and religions? Keep in mind as you move toward this greater understanding that you are only God's tool. God does the real work, and you must trust God's infinite capacity to use you as you are. God has given you the ability to prepare yourself as best you can—that's your responsibility. After that you must let go and turn yourself over to God's guiding Spirit.

GETTING TO KNOW EACH PARTICIPANT

To learn more about your participants, you should design activities, interviews, projects, and journal writing that reveal:

- Their culture.
- Their family life.
- Their past experiences in religious education.
- Their likes and dislikes.
- How they process information.
- Who they consider to be their friends.
- Their role in the community.
- Their dreams and aspirations.
- Words they would use to describe themselves.
- Their favorite sports, hobbies, and crafts.
- Their favorite television programs and music.
- What they would like to change about their lives.

I am reminded of a story by Anthony DeMello about a young minnow who approaches a wise old sturgeon in the ocean and asks where he might learn what water is like. The older fish answers, "Look around you, my child." It is only then that the minnow understands, for until that point he does not recognize that water is the very thing surrounding him. All of us exist within a certain context. We must take it into account when we are planning our time with our participants.

CONTEXT: CIRCLES OF MEANING

If you understand that context is the framework of meaning, you can quickly recognize that we need to discuss context in many areas and on many levels. Strangely enough, building this part of the framework of our planning puzzle creates another puzzle. That's the way context works. Like circles within circles, we can move inward or outward, always finding wider or smaller boundaries. In fact, this can be a very useful exercise.

Draw a circle that represents you.

Now draw the circles that contain you, the ones for family, community, country, and world.

Right away, you are probably having trouble doing this. Even in the simplest example, some circles don't fit completely into other circles. Your church isn't completely surrounded by your community and your community isn't completely surrounded by your church. Perhaps even your family isn't completely surrounded by your community.

Try the same exercise with some of your participants.

Do you have the same circles?

Do you even overlap in the same places?

If your teaching is going to be meaningful to your participants, you must have some understanding of their context. You also need to recognize that your own context creates limitations for you. The popular admonition to "think outside the box" refers to developing ideas that are not limited by our usual boundaries.

A person who comes to a Rite of Christian Initiation of Adults (RCIA) program from a Buddhist background will have different needs than a person who comes from a Baptist background. A person who struggles with the English language might have trouble understanding a verbal presentation that a catechist considers very straightforward. A person who has been abused by a parent may not be reassured by parental images of God. A person who has been in prison may harbor resentment against authority or law. Some participants will have less catechetical experiences than others. The great diversity of contexts can be daunting, but with sensitivity and an open mind, you can meet the challenge!

CONTEXT OF OUR WORLD VIEW

We not only work in the context of our own lives, we teach in the context of our religion and our history. The Israelites wandering in the desert understood things very differently than the Jews who lived in communities where Jesus taught. Yet both celebrated the belief that God was involved in their history. Christians living in American cities have a view of the world that would be completely alien to Jews living in the first century. Yet with the promise of the Spirit given to us by Jesus, we share our own experience of God in our times.

Jesus gave us an alternative view of the world and the people around us. By giving us a new covenant he established a new context for us. It is our responsibility to embrace an ever-widening view of our world.

If we want to communicate effectively within our particular context, we must learn both to listen and to engage in effective dialogue. A quote from Anglican Bishop Kenneth Cragg can inspire us:

> Our first task in approaching another people, another culture, another religion, is to take off our shoes, for the place we are approaching is holy. Else we may find ourselves treading on each other's dreams. More seriously still, we may forget that God was there before our arrival.

THE GOSPEL AND CULTURE

The gospel has already been proclaimed to many different cultures in response to Jesus' instruction: "Go therefore and make disciples of all nations, baptizing them in the name of the Father, and of the Son, and of the Holy Spirit, and teaching them to obey everything that I have commanded you. And remember, I am with you always, to the end of the age" (Matt 28:19–20). The richness of our tradition brings with it a myriad of cultural expressions which can add to our teaching. You will find them in art, music, distinctive food, clothing, dance, and prayer rituals. Yet, culture goes beyond ethnicity and nationalism to include the various contexts and groups to which one belongs.

Culture is deeply embedded within each person. It is defined as the learned and shared values, beliefs, norms, objects, perspectives, language, and history that are transmitted both consciously and unconsciously over time. Though much of culture remains hidden below the surface, it still affects how people view the world, how they act, and how they believe. Most people may not even be aware of all the cultural influences that shape them into unique individuals.

Take time to assess your own culture. What are the circles of influence for you? Remember that cultural groupings are based on different factors, such as age, gender, ability, shared interests, religion, group membership, family, experience, and history. Often we discover our own cultural uniqueness when we meet someone very different from ourselves or when we are placed within unfamiliar surroundings. Being able to share your unique culture with others will not only give you confidence in yourself, but it will open your mind to cultures that are different from your own. As a way of discovering your own cultural heritage ask yourself:

- What is sacred to you?
- What important beliefs do you have?

- What would you want to hand on to other generations?
- What stories, symbols, and objects create meaning for your life?
- Who are your heroes and heroines?
- What prayer forms do you value?

Studying the news in a prayerful manner is a great way to open the minds of your participants to other cultural and political contexts. The seasons and holidays can be used to introduce the context of the liturgical calendar. Developing the theme of forgiveness can be illustrated within the context of friendship and family relationships. The local faith community can be described as part of the larger context of the universal church. Helping your Christian participants to recognize the diversity of human cultural traditions will widen their own contextual circle.

PARISH CONTEXT

Before catechists actually begin to plan the teaching year they need to recognize that they are part of a collaborative catechetical team within a distinctive faith community. Look at your parish mission statement or pastoral plan for catechesis. The director of religious education (DRE) and the principal of the parish school can help you structure your catechetical program so that it is in accordance with the parish's stated mission. Parents and other leaders within the community can also offer advice about the catechetical efforts of the parish.

The text of the *General Directory for Catechesis (GDC)* issued by the Vatican's Congregation for the Clergy in 1997 can be found on the Vatican's website: www.vatican.va. Paragraph 220 of this document clearly states that the responsibility for catechesis resides with the entire faith community, while also acknowledging that catechesis is part of the larger mission of the church to evangelize (*GDC* 220).

- How does your particular parish see itself evangelizing, sharing, and learning about Jesus?
- Is there a particular culture or cultures that exist within your parish community?
- What is unique about the way your parish community understands who they are and practices what they believe?

Every catechist and teacher of religion is connected to this larger dimension of evangelization and will have to address the challenge of inculturation as it is expressed by the *General Directory for Catechesis:* "In light of the Gospel the church must appropriate all the positive values of culture and cultures and reject elements which impede development of the true potential of persons and peoples" (*GDC* 21).

THE *NATIONAL DIRECTORY FOR CATECHESIS* AND THE U.S. CONTEXT

With this task in mind, the U.S. conference of Catholic Bishops published the *National Directory for Catechesis (NDC)* in May 2005 as a companion to the *GDC*. The *NDC* can be purchased online at the U.S. Catholic Bishops' website: www.usccbpublishing.org. One of the purposes of this document is the renewal of catechetical instruction in the United States. Chapter One, *Proclaiming the Gospel in the United States,* outlines our U.S. context: (1) general characteristics of U.S. culture, (2) diversity in U.S. culture, (3) a profile of Catholics in the United States, and (4) family and home in the United States. Among the characteristics of the United States described in this chapter we find: freedom in general, religious freedom, economic freedom, pragmatism, interest in science and technology, globalization, and mobility. All of these characteristics influence our efforts for both evangelization and catechesis in the United States. How does each enhance our efforts? Where does each impede the gospel?

The *NDC* states that "the United States enjoys a rich community life that has been sustained by an emphasis on pluralism and individual freedom" (*NDC* 11B). "At the same time pluralism and individualism pose a challenge for social cohesion in the United States" (*NDC* 10A). Diversity in all areas—cultural, regional, religious, and ethnic—are discussed. We find that the "Catholic population of the United States is more ethnically diverse than a similarly sized Catholic population in any other country in the world" (*NDC* 12A).

The challenge to your catechetical planning process will be "to introduce the real person of Jesus Christ to the real persons of this time and place in history" (*NDC* 14). Introduce your participants to Jesus' story, as found in our scriptures, in a way that makes the Living Word present to them. Help them to enter the scripture stories and look at contemporary issues in the light of gospel values. Ask them to imagine themselves as Jesus' followers in today's context. Our challenge is to foster discipleship of Jesus within the dominant U.S. culture.

AGE APPROPRIATENESS

Participant age level is a significant contextual component in religious education. Systematic catechesis takes a spiral approach, using appropriate methodology to explore the journey of faith at different age levels. It uses scripture and doctrine to deepen religious understanding in a progressive fashion. Adults sometimes become frustrated with a child's lack of understanding: "Do I have to tell you everything?" We now know that children's brains continue to develop through the teen years. Conceptual thinking doesn't become apparent until age thirteen. The religious education that is offered to a child must be different than that provided to an adult. Religious education and faith formation are lifetime pursuits. The catechist doesn't need to teach everything all at once. Rather, each experience should address the immediate needs of the participant and form a foundation for future understanding.

There are many texts and resources that address age-appropriate methodology. Be sure to check the catechist guide of your textbook and read through the background information on growth and development for the level you are teaching.

As people grow, they gain skills and abilities that contribute to the learning process. Very young children need to experience lessons in physically concrete ways, and catechists must recognize the limitations of their motor skill development. Primary grade children focus more on their individual experiences and seek ways to please the teacher in the learning process. As they move into the intermediate grades they become more conscious of others around them and enjoy participating in group activities. Adolescents are better able to search internally for understanding, while remaining very aware of what their peers might think. All real learning is based on experience, whether immediate and hands on, or reflective.

This model of education does not involve pouring content into people as if they were empty vessels waiting to be filled. Such a model relies on memory alone, but true education helps participants grow.

Every lesson at every age level must include three important elements: content, process, and relationship. When you walk away from a lesson feeling good about it, you can probably identify those three components. When you walk away feeling that you missed the mark, it's probably because you missed one of those elements.

Imagine a hamburger with all the fixings. The meat is like the content of the lesson. The processes you use in class are like the fixings that satisfy an individualized taste. The relationships and connections found within the lesson make up the bun that holds it all together so you can eat the whole messy burger. In most hamburgers, the meat is actually the smallest part. But it isn't complete without the bun and the condiments. The processes and the relationships in the classroom are what create the experiences that make learning the fundamental concepts possible.

All people want to be known, understood, and accepted. Based on the work you have done in this chapter, you now have a good foundation to know, understand, and accept your participants for who they are. You just need to communicate with your participants and have them communicate with each other. Because this is religious education, the processes can also be individual or meditative. For your participants, these processes will involve age-appropriate development of their understanding of self, of community, and of God.

3
Setting Goals

It is easy to get frustrated, lost, and fragmented in planning all the details needed for a religious education program. As a result, you can also lose sight of the whole picture you are trying to develop. You might even be tempted to pay attention only to your immediate tasks, forgetting to step back and consider the entire teaching year and the overall needs of a particular group of participants. Such consideration is called long-range planning, and it should be done before you start planning individual lessons. Long-range planning includes:

- Reviewing the textbook's table of contents and units of study to see what topics are covered;
- Determining how the lessons or units progress or build on each other;
- Studying how your resource text, the catechist's guide, and the textbook provide a basic structure to be used within each lesson;
- Devising basic lesson plans;
- Carefully scheduling the lessons of each unit.

This type of planning will help clarify both your purpose in teaching the course and your desired results for the year. Long-range planning also helps to facilitate good time management, making it easier for you to accomplish your teaching goals by the end of the course.

YEAR-LONG GOALS

A goal is a statement of direction in clear, general terms. It is the end result to which all your planning leads. Most goals will take more than a single lesson to attain, so the planning process will usually require establishing numerous smaller objectives that will ultimately lead to final ones. To help yourself begin to think about goals, reflect prayerfully on the following questions:

- How can I create a pleasant learning environment that fosters the growth of my participants' Catholic faith? (Possible answers: By using symbols of the faith within a prayer space. By greeting everyone by name.)
- What spiritual values do the participants bring with them?
- How can I help the participants become more aware of God's goodness?
- How can I facilitate a richer prayer life for the participants?
- How do the families of this community support the participants?

- In what ways can I support more meaningful experiences of worship and the sacraments for the participants?
- How can I help the participants become more aware of Christ's presence in their lives?
- What values and facts about Roman Catholicism are important to both me and the participants? Some possible answers:
  - That the doctrines of the Trinity, incarnation, and resurrection are essential teachings found within the *Catechism of the Catholic Church* (*CCC*[1] 234, 463, 653).
  - That by our baptism we participate in the paschal mystery (*CCC* 654) no matter what our age.
  - That Jesus Christ is completely divine and completely human.
  - That Mary plays a unique role in salvation history as mother of Jesus, the Incarnate One.
  - That in our Sunday liturgy, the celebration of the mass, the bread and wine actually become the body and blood of Christ.

---

1. In order to meet conformity standards set forth by the United States Conference of Catholic Bishops' Committee to Oversee the Use of the Catechism, publishers of catechetical materials must include age-appropriate explanations of essential Church doctrines for each learning level. Remember, the Catechism is not a text to be used in the classroom. Rather, it is a point of reference for those who catechize. Its teachings must be made clear to participants at all levels in language that they can understand. This is one of the essential tasks of a catechist.

After spending some time reflecting on your responses to the above questions, try to answer for yourself the following question.

> What three overall goals do you wish to accomplish with your group of participants this year?
> 1.
>
> 2.
>
> 3.

Answering this will not only help you establish goals for the year, but it will also give you a good sense of your overall purpose for being with your participants. You will then be able to express to them the "what" and the "why" of your teaching year. For example, your goals for the year could be expressed as:

- To help your participants appreciate the goodness of God in creation, and to help them develop their capacity for both traditional and spontaneous prayer.

- To create a loving community that encourages each individual to grow in knowledge of the Catholic faith.
- To recognize Jesus as a friend who leads us to God the Father through the Spirit.
- To enthusiastically share your love of God with your participants by your commitment to planning and preparation, by your support of the families in their primary role of catechesis, by your attentiveness to the word of God found in the scriptures, and by the integration of your participants into the larger parish faith community.

"BACKWARD PLANNING"

Educators today use an approach called "backward planning" that begins with the end in mind and works toward that end. First, establish a goal for the year. Then work backward, always keeping your goal in sight and making sure to accomplish the tasks necessary for achieving that goal.

It is a mistake to look only at our immediate or initial needs—something we might be tempted to do because of a lack of time. Planning only for individual teaching sessions will result in lessons that are isolated from the overall plan of the year.

INTERMEDIATE PLANNING

Divide your year into individual blocks composed of several lessons. Once you have a sense of how the various lessons relate to each other, you will be able to move from lesson to lesson with a greater degree of continuity, and your participants will be able to apply what they have already learned as they advance to a new subject.

Your main task is helping learners grasp concepts and make connections between life and faith. This is an important goal to keep in mind as you work with your participants. With your overall long-range goals in mind, you will be more likely to employ techniques that will weave several lessons together, enabling you to better achieve your teaching objectives.

Repetition is invaluable for enabling participants to firmly retain religious concepts. So make sure you review previous lessons. Also try using familiar music and ritual actions from lesson to lesson. Such techniques foster a sense of consistency and repetition. They allow everyone to become familiar with the process and take ownership of their learning experience.

Read through one of the lesson outlines to better understand the approach that your particular textbook uses. Look for background material that can assist you in your preparation. Compare the scope and sequence charts for your grade level with those of other grade levels. Studying both your text and your scope and sequence charts will help you get a better sense of the course content and the textbook resources.

IMMEDIATE PLANNING STEPS

Now it is finally time to move on to more immediate planning of an individual lesson. You will find detailed steps for immediate planning in Chapter Five. The resource section of your textbook should have objectives written for each individual lesson. An objective differs from the goal in that it is a specific, time-oriented and realistic statement of what is going to be accomplished, who is going to do it, for whom, when, and how. Objectives need to be observable, quantifiable, and measurable so that you can easily evaluate whether or not an objective has been accomplished. Objective statements explicitly state what the participant must do to accomplish the objective. For example, "At the end of a unit on covenant the participants should be able to summarize the key events in the story of Abraham and Sarah; identify the importance of trust in covenant relationships; and recognize Abraham, Sarah, and Mary as models of faith and trust." Objectives written in this style are also referred to as learning outcomes.

Strategies are action steps that help the participant reach the learning objective for a particular lesson. A plan consists of a set of strategies for progressively achieving an objective. Strategies are part of the immediate planning for a lesson. In order to determine the progression of strategies you must examine all the lessons within a unit of study.

Variety of Strategies and Methods

Dale's Cone of Learning divides activities into three categories: symbolizing, observing, and doing. The doing group is at the bottom of the cone and includes direct experiences such as games, role playing, models, drama, and demonstrations. The middle of the cone includes the observing activities: field trips, exhibits, films, videos, audio recordings, and pictures or slides. The top of the cone contains the symbolizing group. These are visual symbols, including maps, drawings, charts, graphs, chalkboards, and bulletins. At the tip of the cone are verbal

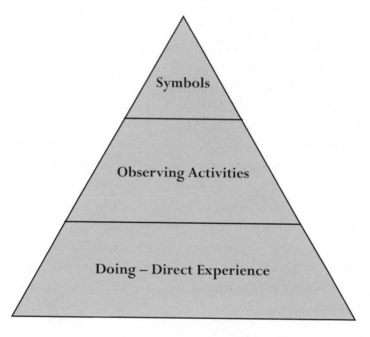

symbols such as words used in reading, discussing, and lectures. Participation increases as you move to the bottom of the cone, and Dale's premise is that the greater degree of participation, the more effective the learning experience. Of course these activities do not stand alone. In fact, their effectiveness comes from correlation or integration with one another.

It is essential that you use a variety of activities, strategies, and techniques in your planning. Keep in mind that the participants will typically remember:

- 90% of what they DO.
- 70% of what they SAY.
- 50% of what they both SEE *and* HEAR.
- 30% of what they SEE.
- 20% of what they HEAR.
- 10% of what they READ.

Incorporating different activities, strategies, and techniques into your lessons will also allow you to address the variety of learning styles within each group.

The need for a variety of methods is acknowledged in the *General Directory for Catechesis*: "Perfect fidelity to Catholic doctrine is compatible with a rich diversity of presentation (*GDC* 122)....The variety of methods is a sign of life and richness as well as a demonstration of respect for those to whom catechesis is addressed" (*GDC* 148).

The process of learning in catechesis is both progressive and holistic. It follows a plan that recognizes the development of the person in receiving the Good News of salvation.

Genuine catechesis encourages a climate of listening, of thanksgiving, and of prayer. It looks to the free response of persons and it promotes active participation among those to be catechized (*GDC* 145).

Objectives that involve the whole person in the learning process are cognitive, affective, and behavioral. It is interesting to note how all three objectives are part of the response to the familiar Baltimore Catechism question, "Why did God make you?" The traditional response is, "God made me *to know, to love, and to serve* him in this world, and to be happy with him in the next."

Cognitive objectives help us to know God and be able to share the Good News with others. Affective objectives deal with our feelings and emotions in order for us to recognize God's love for us and respond—to love God. Behavioral objectives help us to put into practice ways in which we share God's love with others—to serve. Discipleship demands that all three objectives become part of our learning process and that we engage head, heart, and hands through our many strategies.

CATECHESIS IS MORE THAN TEACHING

As you plan your lessons, remember that catechesis differs from regular teaching in that "the definitive aim of catechesis is to put people not only in touch, but also in communion and intimacy, with Jesus Christ" (*GDC* 80). It is not only knowing about Jesus' life, teaching, death, and resurrection, but, more importantly, developing a personal relationship with Jesus Christ. All goals and objectives created for your teaching year will then become part of evangelizing efforts and the formation of disciples of Jesus Christ.

Catechesis has six fundamental tasks. The *National Directory for Catechesis* (*NDC* 20) describes these as follows:

1. Catechesis promotes knowledge of the faith.
2. Catechesis promotes understanding of the meaning of the liturgy and the sacraments.
3. Catechesis promotes moral formation in Jesus Christ.
4. Catechesis teaches the Christian how to pray with Christ.
5. Catechesis prepares the Christian to live in community and to participate actively in the life and mission of the Church.
6. Catechesis promotes a missionary spirit that prepares the faithful to be present as Christians in society.

These tasks are interrelated. For example, our participation in the sacraments strengthens us to live a moral life. Growing in knowledge of our faith prepares us for mission and enables us to explain our faith to others. The process of education for community life is one of apprenticeship in which your class and the whole of the parish community are involved. It involves learning (1) a spirit of simplicity and humility, (2) solicitude for "the least," (3) concern for the alienated, (4) fraternal correction, and (5) mutual forgiveness.

PROCESS OF THE CATECHUMENAL MODEL

The *GDC* (90) and the *NDC* (35D) both state that "the baptismal catechumenate is the source of inspiration for all catechesis." This inspiration can be found within the process of the Rite of Christian Initiation of Adults (RCIA). RCIA includes the following elements:

- Beginning the gradual process of catechetical formation at whatever place people are in their lives.
- Acknowledging the reality of different stages or periods of growth and conversion.
- Focusing on word and sacrament.
- Involving the community in the process.
- Bringing individuals into the liturgical body.
- Calling us continually into a deeper embrace of the paschal mystery and transformation of our life.

These elements are important not only for pre-baptismal catechesis but also for post-baptismal catechesis.

4

Organizing Your Calendar and Planning Lessons

CALENDARS

Chapter 1 suggested daily and weekly "time wheels" to help you identify the best time for planning. Once you have a good sense of your daily and weekly schedules, you can transfer this information to your calendar.

There are several kinds of calendars, including eighteen-month academic calendars (July through December of the next year), month-at-a-glance calendars, week-at-a-glance calendars, daily schedules, and so forth. Select one that will help you keep track of the significant dates for your class. Make sure your lesson-planning calendar is separate from your household calendar. It shouldn't be cluttered up with activities that are not related to your catechetical program.

Include in the calendar all holy days, sacrament dates, liturgies, and reconciliation services. Mark all holidays and back-to-school nights. Include major scheduled events from the parish calendar so you can avoid scheduling conflicts with other parish organizations. Mark on your calendar any scheduled in-service meetings and dates when lessons will not be held. Once you have met with your class you can add their birth dates to your calendar. Finally, include any significant personal dates and events that will affect your time and commitment.

Liturgical Calendar

It is also a good idea to become acquainted with the liturgical calendar, which begins with the First Sunday of Advent. This calendar moves through the Advent season, the Christmas season, a short period of Ordinary time, the Lenten season, the Triduum (three days), the Easter season, Pentecost, and a long stretch through the summer months of Ordinary time. Each year, Liturgy Training Publications (http://www.ltp.org) publishes a poster size (26" by 26") colored graphic of the Catholic liturgical calendar.

Those teaching from the lectionary will find it necessary to prepare for the readings in advance. The United States Conference of Catholic Bishops offers the lectionary readings on their website: http://www.usccb.org /nab/index.htm.

Two excellent lectionary sources include *Breaking Open the Lectionary* by Margaret Nutting Ralph and *Exploring the Sunday Lectionary: A Teenager's Guide to the Readings* by Sandy Rigsby and Steve Mason, both published by Paulist Press (www.paulistpress.com). Each of these publications comes in three volumes, for liturgical years A, B, and C. *Living*

Liturgy, published by Liturgical Press (www.litpress.org), also contains Sunday readings.

Peter Malone, MSC, and Rose Pacatte, FSP, have created a movie lectionary resource titled *Lights Camera... FAITH! A Movie Lover's Guide to Scripture*, for cycles A, B, and C (Pauline Books & Media, 50 Saint Pauls Avenue, Boston, MA 02130, 1-800-876-4463, www.pauline.org). This three-part series brings together faith and life in a unique approach to the lectionary. Each Sunday's readings are seen through the lens of a particular movie that highlights themes or issues emphasized in the gospel.

Magnificat (PO Box 91 Spencerville MD 20868-9978, 1-800-317-6689) and *Living with Christ* (PO Box 6001, Mystic CT 06355-6001, 1-800-321-0411) publish monthly booklets containing both weekday and Sunday readings.

Planning ahead for the Sunday readings will help you meet the challenge of the *NDC* to integrate "the liturgical rites and symbols, liturgical celebrations, and the liturgical year into the catechetical process."

Academic Calendar

Each September issue of *Catechist* magazine contains a removable "Catechist Class Record and Planning Guide," a calendar-style planning guide for the September to May academic year. It identifies the weekly scripture readings and other important dates. The magazine also offers monthly articles that address seasonally pertinent topics.

You can reach *Catechist* magazine at 1-800-523-4625 or http://www.catechist.com.

Refer to your calendar frequently! It is an essential tool for keeping in mind the context of your teaching.

PLANNING LESSONS

In order to feel comfortable presenting material for a lesson, there are several immediate planning steps to take. Keep in mind that for every hour you spend teaching you will have to spend more than an hour preparing. A typical outline for planning a lesson should include:

- The lesson title.
- The goal.
- Learning objectives.
- Each part of the catechetical process.
- Detailed strategies, activities, and questions for the various parts of the lesson.
- Prayer experience.
- List of materials needed.
- Family involvement and home assignment.
- Evaluation.

Even if you have been provided with the script of the lessons you will be teaching during the year, it is best to view these as planning templates rather than the final product. These templates will provide you with useful information and a helpful structure, while you can still make the teaching session your own, allowing your lessons to come alive for your particular group of participants.

Planning Steps

- *Step 1:* At least one week prior to the actual lesson, *read and review the lesson plan* and the suggested activities for your topic. See how the lesson fits within the unit. Scan the lesson that follows the one you are presently planning. Sometimes it is necessary to combine lessons or omit some of the suggested activities due to time constraints. Ask yourself, what are the "signs of the times" in the lives of the participants that relate to the subject of the lesson?

- *Step 2:* Several days before the class, set aside at least an hour to finalize your actual plan for the lesson. *Create an outline for the lesson.* Begin by stating your goal. You may use one suggested by your textbook and adjust it as necessary for your specific situation. (See chapter 3: Setting Goals for a discussion of goals and objectives. Remember, a goal is something you wish to accomplish by the end of a lesson or a series of lessons. Objectives are the intermediate tasks that must be accomplished in order to reach a particular goal.) If you planned goals and objectives as part of your yearly plan, this is the time to review them and incorporate them into the specific lesson. If your text or resource book does not identify goals and objectives, you need to develop them for yourself. Not only will this help you stay on track during your lesson, but it will also foster an ongoing sense of direction and will allow you to recognize what you have accomplished.

- *Step 3: Establish objectives for the participants* for each part of the lesson. Write the objectives in a way that indicates exactly what the participants are expected to accomplish. Keep in mind that sometimes you need to be very flexible. If your objectives are defined in terms of your goals, you will be able to stay on track even if your program takes an unexpected turn. Sometimes a participant will raise a question that is so important it must be addressed, regardless of what you have planned for the lesson. One of my participants once said "Scientists don't believe in God, do they?" This subject didn't fit into that session's lesson plan, but the ensuing discussion did contribute to the catechetical goal of "exploring our relationship with God."

- *Step 4: Plan the strategies or activities* that will help the participants to reach the objectives established above. Vary your activities in order to respond to the different learning styles of your participants. Never perform an activity just to pass the time. Activities must support the lesson and help the participants achieve the established objectives. Always bring more teaching material than you actually plan to use for the lesson, just in case a fifteen-minute activity ends up taking only five minutes. At the same time, you should develop ways to shorten activities in case they turn out to take longer than you expected. You can do this by focusing on the objective of the activity and then identifying its essential and nonessential elements. With experience you will become proficient at planning your lessons to fit the allotted time. Always remember to be flexible!

- *Step 5: Make a list of materials* needed for the lesson and determine where and when you will be able to obtain all of the necessary supplies and equipment. Identify any people you will need to contact for supplies. Do this earlier than you think you need to. Planning ahead is a good way to avoid the stress of the unexpected.
- *Step 6: Evaluation is the final step,* performed after the teaching session is over. Make a note of what worked and what didn't. How well did the strategies support the different objectives? How long did it actually take to do some of the activities? What still needs attention in the next lesson? Retain all prepared materials for possible use in upcoming lessons. This will save you future preparation time.

An outline is essential. In preparing an outline—even for material that is already scripted in your text—you are engaging with your class material. Having an outline will give you the confidence to allow a discussion to develop freely without losing control of the overall presentation.

If you are planning a complex or difficult lesson, you can note the different elements on sticky notes and arrange them until you are satisfied with the structure and flow of the lesson. Or you can draw a chart. Whatever method you use, consider writing the major headings of the final outline onto 4"x 6" index cards. The cards will not contain the details of your plan, but they are a convenient way to keep track of where you are during the teaching session.

The Art of Questioning

Teachers must develop the art of questioning. Prepare engaging and meaningful questions for your participants. Ask straightforward, concrete questions first, especially with children, to bring the participants into the context of the lesson. After that you can ask for opinions, points of view, or personal life experiences. You should have at least two or three open-ended questions to get you started. Telling people what's going on isn't nearly as important as asking good questions. Once participants start responding to questions, they become engaged and the learning process becomes theirs, not yours. This is the whole sense of discovery and dialogue that you are trying to facilitate as a catechist. Questioning is an essential teaching tool.

There are a variety of question styles that promote greater class participation. Asking a question of each participant, one at a time, will let you survey class opinion on a topic. If a participant asks a question, you can boomerang it back to the class and solicit possible answers. Others can be drawn into the discussion by simply asking, "Can anyone else add to that point?" Remember to allow time for listeners to formulate responses. Repeat or rephrase a question if the class does not seem to understand what you are asking. Avoid cutting off responses by asking another question too quickly. Try not to ask simple yes or no questions.

Good teachers know the value of questions. In our culture, questions are often used for evaluation and competition, as in quizzes and exams. However, if you understand the cultural context of your participants, you can use questions to affirm their self-esteem and make them feel comfortable about participating in discussions.

From kindergarten through graduate school, participants are asked to prove themselves. At every level, participants must compete and be good enough to move on to the next grade. The message is that participants are expected to know the answers every time they are asked a question. So instead of becoming a teaching tool, questions sometimes lead participants to think that they are expected to know everything. In catechesis, this all-knowing attitude does not really work. Even in primary grades children complain that they are "dumb" because they can't answer all the questions. No one likes to look dumb because they might get an answer wrong.

So how can you make sure your participants will have a chance to get the right answer without being embarrassed? The solution to this is fairly simple, but it requires preparation and discipline. For any questions that are intended to elicit content (as opposed to opinion or experience), *make sure the answers are already available.* How? You could have the answers on display around the room or on materials that you have handed out to the participants. Or you might state the answers verbally just before you ask the question. It's also a good idea to have participants work in groups so they can help each other and answer questions as a team. Avoid putting individuals on the spot. To prevent a few "smart" or more outgoing people from dominating the class, try not to ask for volunteers.

You can use the following starters when formulating questions:

- Who is the person who…?
- What can you tell me about…?
- Can you think of a way to…?
- How do you feel when…?
- Do you agree with…Why? or Why not?
- What do you think Jesus meant by…?
- Have you ever wondered…?
- Can you give an example of…?
- What did you hear…?

As you write your questions, keep in mind the characteristics of a good question:

- Clear—avoids technical language.
- Concisely stated.

- Appropriate to the age level of the participants.
- Requires reflection on the participants' own experiences.
- Requires an extended answer, not just yes or no.
- Promotes critical thinking—may have more than one answer.
- Addresses one specific topic.
- Flows from the previous question and into the next one.

Jesus' Questions

Throughout the gospels, Jesus used questions to engage his listeners and help them apply his message to their own lives. Here are a few examples that demonstrate how Jesus' questions brought his message to life, not only in his time but also for us today.

- "For if you love those who love you, what reward do you have?" (Matt 5:46).
- "Look at the birds of the air...Are you not of more value than they? And can any of you by worrying add a single hour to your span of life?" (Matt 6:26-27).
- Introducing the parable of the mustard seed he asks, "What is the kingdom of God like? And to what shall I compare it?" (Luke 13:18).
- To illustrate God's joy over one repentant sinner, Jesus asks. "Which one of you, having a hundred sheep and losing one of them, does not leave the

ninety-nine in the wilderness and go after the one that is lost until he finds it? (Luke 15:4) "Or what woman having ten silver coins, if she loses one of them, does not light a lamp, sweep the house, and search carefully until she finds it?" (Luke 15:8).

- "For what will it profit them to gain the whole world and forfeit their life? Indeed, what can they give in return for their life?" (Mark 8:36–37).

Stepping Back

At this point, try to analyze your approach to lesson planning.

- What time of the day do you plan? Is this the best time?
- Where do you do your planning? Is this the best place?
- What kinds of learning activities do you favor in your plans? Why?
- Do you take the time to write your questions for each part of the lesson?
- Do you start your planning with prayer, relying on the Spirit for guidance?
- What is one unique, helpful technique you have used?
- What new teaching technique would you like to try?
- Is there someone with whom you can exchange teaching strategies?

This chapter addressed the skill of lesson planning and the art of questioning. But more particularly, it emphasized the catechist's use of these skills to design an effective teaching plan. It is recommended that you return to this chapter after you have taught several lessons so that you can review its content in the light of your teaching experience. Remember, you the catechist are essential to the catechetical learning process. The *General Directory for Catechesis* (156) describes your importance in this way: "No methodology, no matter how well tested, can dispense with the person of the catechist in every phrase of the catechetical process. The charism given by the Spirit, a solid spirituality and transparent witness of life, constitutes the soul of every method."

5
Gathering Resources

Your primary resources as a catechist are you, your teaching text, and scripture. The previous chapters have offered suggestions to develop these three essential resources. There are many other resources that can provide ideas, materials, references, and media to assist your planning process and that can be effectively incorporated into your lesson plans. In this chapter we will look at some additional resources.

SUPPLY BOX

Create a supply box that contains all of the items you might need for your activities. The box or container should be easy to carry and big enough for all the items. It can contain such things as scissors, pencils, pens, white glue, glue sticks, crayons, markers, paper clips, stapler, staples, pins, blue tape (safe for walls), transparent tape, sticky notes, paper, colored construction paper, ruler, name tags, envelopes, stickers, labels, string, yarn, pipe cleaners, and so on. Of course, the contents of your box will vary with the age level of your class.

ENVIRONMENT

A Bible, candles, cloth, incense, holy cards, icons, cross, wheat, grapes, book stand, chimes, and candlesticks are just some of the religious symbols you might use from week to week in your prayer space. The prayer space can be changed each week to highlight the topic of the lesson or the liturgical season. Colored cloth is especially helpful for marking Advent (bluish purple), Ordinary time (green), and Lent (purple). Natural objects such as flowers, leaves, rocks, water, branches, pumpkins, gourds, holly, earth, sand, and cactus are all part of God's wonderful creation and can be used in lessons. Keep your eyes open for items that will enhance your catechetical environment.

STORIES AND SAINTS

Each resource text usually has stories that can be used with your lessons. Children's books with beautiful illustrations are another resource. *Brother Eagle, Sister Sky,* illustrated by Susan Jeffers, provides a good example of a children's book whose theme has catechetical resonances, touching as it does upon creation, stewardship, unity, and care for our environment. Stories of the lives of the saints are also recommended. Two websites with very good information on the saints are http://www.catholic.org/saints/ or http://www.americancatholic.org/Features/SaintofDay/.

MUSIC

Music can be a vital part of catechetics, especially for young children, who enjoy singing. Music can engage participants at the levels of body, mind, and spirit, and even help them grasp certain concepts. Music can also be used as a background for meditation and prayer. Even contemporary music can help make the connection between life and faith. For example, Josh Groban's rendition of "You Raise Me Up" speaks of resurrection and dependence in our troubled times.

Check with the publisher of your textbook to see if it offers a music CD that correlates with the text. Some well-known distributors of sacred music are:

- OCP Publications (5536 NE Hassalo, Portland, OR 97213, 1-800-548-8749, www.ocp.org)
- GIA Publications (7404 South Mason Ave, Chicago IL, 60638, 1-800-442-1358, www.giamusic.com)
- World Library Publications (WLP, 3708 River Road, Suite 400, Franklin Park, IL 60131, 1-800-566-6150, www.wlpmusic.com)

A resource to help you understand the music that appeals to teens can be found at Corner Stone Media, Inc. (P.O. Box 6236, Santa Rosa, CA 95406, 707-542-8273, www.cornerstonemedia.org). They offer free resources on their website and a review in "Top Music Countdown."

The music that young people listen to everyday can spark dialogue about values and relationships.

LEARNING ACTIVITIES

Lessons can include various activities, such as arts and crafts projects, role playing, puzzles, games, and other projects that encourage self-expression. To get ideas, consult with your fellow catechists and the DRE. Use activity books and the Internet. Write down new ideas on index cards to try out in class. Some of the activities will become favorites for both you and the participants.

MEDIA

When this word is used, people tend to think of digital or electronic media, videos, DVDs, and CDs. But the word also refers to anything that conveys a message. Clearly each catechist is an important medium. Catechists communicate their message by the way they look and respond to their participants. Evaluate yourself as a medium for the message of Jesus Christ. What does your appearance say? What nonverbal message is conveyed by your facial expressions? Do you smile or frown? Do you greet and address each person by name? (Doing so communicates that you care and that your participants are uniquely important to you.) How does God's love shine through you?

Remember not to overlook the quiet participant who tends to remain in the background. Be conscious of your body language. Keeping your hands on your hips, crossing your arms, having a puzzled look on your face—such postures might be interpreted by participants to mean that you are unapproachable or unsympathetic. Give participants a chance to talk about current events or what is happening in their lives at the beginning of the class. This will let them know that their lives are an important part of the teaching session. God loves each one of your participants and wants to be part of their everyday lives. Make sure you communicate that to them both verbally and nonverbally.

Charts, posters, PowerPoint, photos, symbols, graphic designs, and other visual and print media will make your presentations more effective. Probably eighty-five percent of participants are "visual participants"—that is, they benefit more from visual than from auditory presentations. So it's a good idea to remove anything that clutters your teaching space so that your participants can focus more easily. Also be aware that participants of all ages are fascinated by books with interesting pictures and illustrations. Whenever you can, use illustrations and charts to display the information that you are teaching. If participants can see the written word, they can better assimilate the information. A flip chart is an effective tool for writing or drawing concepts, because you can later tape the information around the room for review.

The Vatican's 1991 pastoral instruction *On Social Communications* states that "the use of media is now essential in evangelization and catechesis." This idea is reiterated in #69 of the *National Directory for Catechesis (Communications, Technology and Catechesis)*:

While the developments in communication technology present challenges and potential problems for catechetical leaders and catechists, they also present many promising opportunities to proclaim the message of Jesus Christ in engaging new ways to vast numbers of people who might otherwise never hear it. They provide a new and more effective forum for proclaiming the Gospel to all nations and all people... The communications media are useful catechetical tools, but those who use them must be aware that they have the power to shape the environment and that they are therefore multidimensional catechetical resources. Among the contemporary means of communication are the electronic media (television, radio, films, audio- and videocassettes, DVDs, compact discs, and an entire range of other audiovisual aids); the print media (newspapers, magazines, books, pamphlets, and parish bulletins); and computer-related media (the Internet, CD-ROMs, distance-learning materials, and interactive software programs)....Contemporary communications media do not merely transmit information; they generate visual, audible, emotional, and, in some cases, entirely virtual experiences for individuals and communities. Well-planned catechesis must employ these media so that the message of Jesus Christ can be effectively communicated in the real circumstances and culture of those who seek him.

Acquiring and operating the equipment necessary for using electronic media can be challenging, as can be the task of finding appropriate media to begin with. Some catechists are tempted to give up on electronic media altogether—but this is a mistake. First, you should find out what your text recommends as appropriate media. Then ask your coordinator or the DRE what media and equipment are available in the parish. Check the public library for media pieces. Your diocesan media center will also be able to make recommendations and guide you to appropriate materials. Visit the National Association of Catechetical Media Professionals (NACMP) at www.nacmp.org.

Always make sure the equipment is working properly before class begins. Young participants are more likely to misbehave when the teacher is preoccupied with a malfunctioning piece of equipment. Older participants will become bored and disengaged during such "down time," when the focus of the class has become operating equipment rather than faith formation.

THE UNITED STATES COUNCIL OF CATHOLIC BISHOPS (USCCB)

The USCCB not only publishes the *Catechism of the Catholic Church,* but also a number of essential English and Spanish language documents that will be of interest to catechists. Among these are the *National Directory for Catechesis* and related publications. They have an online catalog listing all of their publications. They can be reached at: USCCB Publishing, 3211 Fourth Street NE, Washington, DC 20017; Toll free: 800-235-8722; Fax: 202-722-8709; Web: www.usccbpublishing.org; Customer Service: CSS@usccb.org.

ONLINE INTERNET RESOURCES

The Internet is another source of resources. In addition to printed material, publishers of catechetical resources today offer interactive online games, evaluative quizzes, and family-friendly materials. Here are a few Internet home pages of catechetical publishers:

Paulist Press	http://www.paulistpress.com
Harcourt Religion Publishers	http://harcourtreligion.com
Loyola Press	http://www.findinggod.com
RCL Benziger	http://www.rclbenziger.com
William H. Sadlier, Inc	http://www.sadlier.com

Be sure to look up the publisher whose text you are currently using for their online support of your ministry.

Check out Puzzlemaker at http://puzzlemaker.school.discovery.com to create your own puzzles online. You can find free clip art from Microsoft at http://office.microsoft.com/clipart and a PowerPoint template for class rules at http://office.microsoft.com/en-us/templates/TC063649261033.aspx. If you are looking for "free stuff," such as Christian bookmarks, clip art, poetry, and posters, go to http://www. christianfreebies.com. The website of *Our Sunday Visitor,* http://www.osv.com/teachingcatholicyouth/catechistknowhow.asp, hosts "Teaching Catholic Kids," which offers resources for catechists and includes activities and prayer services for kids. These are just a few of the websites available. Spend an afternoon searching and you will find quite a few more links!

If you have really gotten hooked by the Internet and wish to spend some time setting up your own site for your catechetical class, SchoolNotes, http://www.schoolnotes.com, offers web hosting for teachers. Through this free community service, you can create notes for your class and information for parents and post them on the web in seconds. Participants and parents can view your website by entering your school ZIP code. Be sure to find out what can be added to your parish and school websites.

6
Taking Time for Prayer

A living spirituality is essential to the task of teaching and ministering. This work is God's work, and a catechist must leave room for the Spirit to function. The ministry of sharing the mysteries of God demands time spent in prayer. Before class you might want to center yourself and reflect on your objectives. Set aside some quiet time when you won't be rushed or worried about your preparations. Ask the Spirit to make you a channel for God's word and a living source of faith for all of your participants.

In addressing the community at Corinth, Paul asks, "What then is Apollos? What is Paul? Servants through whom you came to believe, as the Lord assigned to each. I planted, Apollos watered, but God gave the growth" (1 Cor 3:5–6). That growth is for us as well as our participants. We join in the weekly celebration of Eucharist, reflect on God's word throughout our week, and daily focus our efforts to speak with God through formal and spontaneous prayer or silent meditation. Prayer and spirituality are our wholehearted yes to the mystery of God seeking us.

Saying yes to God and agreeing to accept the role of catechist places demands on your time and requires planning and preparation. The willingness to be an instrument of God's love for others also calls you to spend regular time in prayer, attending the Sunday liturgy with the community, and participating in the sacraments. Prayer will support your ministry in many ways. As you grow and learn, you will become more effective in your role as a catechist and teacher. With experience you will learn what works, what needs to change, what your strengths are, and where you need to improve.

GOD'S PROVIDENCE

Once I was planning a Lenten lesson for adults. I wanted to create an environment that reflected the season in a stark and simple way. One early morning as I set out in the dark to meet my walking partner I stumbled upon a very huge, barren branch with prickly thorns. I had no idea how it got there because no tree was nearby. But immediately I saw how it might contribute to a Lenten environment. After carrying it back to my home, I had a truck deliver it to the meeting place, where it was set within a large clay pot. I thanked God for the surprise gift.

God is generous with surprises that help catechists to be effective. They may come from nature, the "signs of our times," or even the words of friends and family. Being attentive to possibilities takes an effort on your part to listen to what God has to offer in the world and with the community of believers. A peaceful mind is more likely to see and hear these marvelous possibilities. Minds that are cluttered with worry or with concern about preparedness can often miss these opportunities. Practice centering prayer in order to unclutter your life and enter into God's peace.

Before each class, set aside some time to quietly visualize how your lesson will proceed. Conclude with a brief prayer for the guidance of the Spirit. Ask God to help you connect the Divine Word with the lives of your participants. As you become a person of prayer, you will be more comfortable in leading others in prayer.

Here is a short Trinitarian prayer. Post it on your refrigerator, mirror, or planning calendar so that it will be handy for you to recite daily.

God, our loving Father,
You created a world filled with beauty and wonder.
Help me to inspire others to respect and hold all life as precious.
Jesus, our Redeemer,
You call us to forgiveness, reconciliation, and compassion.
Show me how to give witness to others
Through acts and attitudes of generosity and kindness.
Spirit of holiness and truth,
You urge us to hope and challenge us to love.
Give me the strength to live a life dedicated to justice and mercy.
In communion with you—
Father, Son, and Holy Spirit—
I pray today especially for—
Amen.

You will find several Internet sites that offer a daily prayer reflection. "Sacred Space" at http://www.sacredspace.ie is a site run by Irish Jesuits in several languages. It is not just a collection of prayers, but a practical prayer experience. Besides a daily meditation, you will find directions for body prayer, breathing, and listening to God. The De La Salle Brothers also have a site with daily prayer reflections at http://www.prayingeachday.org/reflect.html.

PRAYING WITH SCRIPTURE

Both the daily lectionary readings at http://www.nccbuscc.org/nab/ and the Liturgy of the Hours at http://www.liturgyhours.org will give you a way to pray with the larger church. Practice the steps of *Lectio Divina*, an ancient Christian style of prayer, with the daily readings or the Gospel. First, *read* the scripture prayerfully. Next, *think* about what struck you most as you read this passage and why. Then *speak* to God about your thoughts. The last step is to simply rest in God's presence with an open mind and an open heart to *listen* to God's response. You can end your reflection by praying the Lord's Prayer slowly and reverently.

PRAY WITH YOUR PARTICIPANTS

Always make prayer with your class a priority. Pray at the beginning, middle, or end of each teaching session. Involve the participants in the prayer, not only through memorized prayer, but also with music and meaningful ritual actions. Challenge them to pray daily and invite them to join the community regularly at the Sunday liturgy. Help them to recognize that "where two or three are gathered in Christ's name," Christ is present. Help them recognize that God speaks to us through all of creation. Let them experience prayer as blessing, adoration, praise, thanksgiving, petition, and intercession.

Besides making time for prayer in your life and in class, determine areas in which you need additional formation. The *NDC* 55C suggests that catechists continue their formation through frequent reception of the sacraments (especially Eucharist and reconciliation), spiritual direction, and continued study of the faith. Search out retreats and conferences that offer opportunities to grow not just spiritually, but also in terms of pedagogy and methodology. Such training must be ongoing, as society, teaching methods, and culture continue to change.

What exactly will you gain from all your preparation and teaching? You will be energized by the experience and will find that your faith grows along with your participants. You might not know exactly how God touches the lives of your participants at the time you are with them, but with prayer you can know God in your own life and share that experience with others.

Appendix
Evaluation and Feedback

All good planning requires honest evaluation. Take the time immediately after a lesson to ask the following questions:

- Was the class able to meet the learning objectives? How do you know?
- What would you change in the lesson?
- What worked well enough to be used again?
- What areas still need to be developed for a greater understanding?
- How appropriate and effective were the methods used?
- Were all of the participants involved in the lesson?
- How will you review this lesson in the future lessons?

In addition, consider administering informal assessments to your participants. Make it clear these are not tests but are simply ways of gathering information that will improve your role as a catechist. Talk to your participants about how they feel or act after a lesson. Ask them to answer some open-ended questions, either orally or in writing. For example:

Today I learned

_____.

One thing I hope we will do again

_____.

What I remember about today's class

_____.

I especially liked

_____.

What helped me the most today was

_____.

After today's class I can share with my family

_____.

Following the evaluation, move on to planning the next lesson. Remember the six tasks of catechesis as stated in chapter 3. Not all the tasks can be attended to at the same time. It's a process that flows and connects, much like weaving strands into tapestry. Each task and each teaching session should contribute in its own way to the ultimate goal of all of catechesis, which is the conversion of the human person to Jesus Christ.

With prayer as an essential element in your planning, God's grace will shine through all that you do. Knowing that success depends not just on your own efforts, you can continue to grow in confidence. Through you, the Spirit will transform lives. We plant the seeds, we water the soil, but God causes the growth.

OTHER BOOKS IN THIS SERIES

Connecting with Parents
Mary Twomey Spollen

Teaching the Faith
Kim Duty

Praying with Young People
Maureen Gallagher